Science Mind Benders®
Animals

Science Mind Benders products available in print or eBook form:

Animals • Insects

Written by
Ashley Fleming, M.Ed.

Edited by
Michael Baker
Heather Hiveley

Graphics by
Scott Slyter

THE CRITICAL THINKING CO.™
www.CriticalThinking.com
Phone: 800-458-4849 • Fax: 541-756-1758
1991 Sherman Ave., Suite 200 • North Bend • OR 97459
ISBN 978-1-60144-987-0

Printed in the United States of America by Gasch Printing, Odenton, MD (July 2021)

TABLE OF CONTENTS

Important Information!

Science Mind Bender® books teach young students important scientific terms and problem-solving skills using interesting animals. Most of these scientific terms are taught at a much older age, so these lessons and activities are designed for use with a parent or teacher—they are not designed for independent student work. This is also a book that most students will enjoy, but find challenging. For these reasons, many students are open to working through the book more than once.

Students working through these activities will often become curious about the interesting animals in the pictures. This is a great opportunity to introduce some research skills, so students learn how easy it is to find answers to their questions.

Before beginning the first lesson, it is important to work students through the practice problem, so they learn the importance of marking false answers in the Mind Bender® activities. Students who do not mark the false answers will find the Mind Benders® much more challenging.

HOW TO USE A CHART

Each Mind Benders® puzzle gives you a chart and a set of clues. Read the clues very carefully and mark each space yes "X" or no "–" in the chart. Many students make the mistake of just marking "yes" answers in the chart. This makes the puzzles harder to solve since "no" answers sometimes lead you to the "yes" answer.

Example:

A girl, a boy, and their dad have their own pets. Use the clues and chart to find each one's pet.

1. The boy's pet and the dad's pet have legs.
2. The dad's pet likes to sit on his shoulder.

How to Solve:

1. Read clue 1. Look at each of the pets shown at the top of the chart. The bird and the horse have legs, but the snake does not, so the bird and the horse belong to the boy and the dad. If the bird and horse belong to the boy and the dad, the snake must belong to the girl.

2. Mark your answers on the chart. Draw X for yes in the box under the snake in the girl's row. Draw – for no in the other two boxes under the snake and in the other two boxes in the girl's row. Look at your chart; it shows the snake belongs to the girl, not to the boy or the dad.

3. Read clue 2. Could a bird sit on the dad's shoulder? Could a horse sit on the dad's shoulder? This clue tells us that the dad's pet is the bird.
4. Mark your answers on the chart. Draw X for yes in the box under the bird in the dad's row. Draw – for no in the other empty box under the bird and in the other empty box in the dad's row. This means that the bird belongs to the dad, not to the boy.

5. Look at the chart. If the snake belongs to the girl and the bird belongs to the dad, then the horse must belong to the boy. Draw X for yes in the last empty box.

Vertebrates and Invertebrates

Touch your elbow and your knee. Feel those hard things? Those are your bones! Feel the bones down the middle of your back. Those back bones are called your spine, or **vertebrae**. You are a vertebrate!

A **vertebrate** is an animal that has a backbone inside its body.

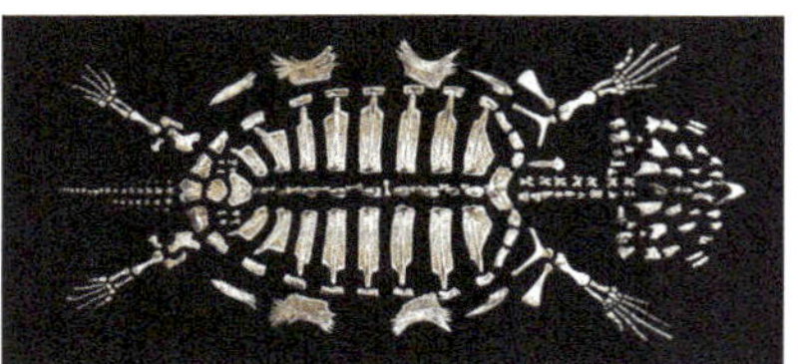

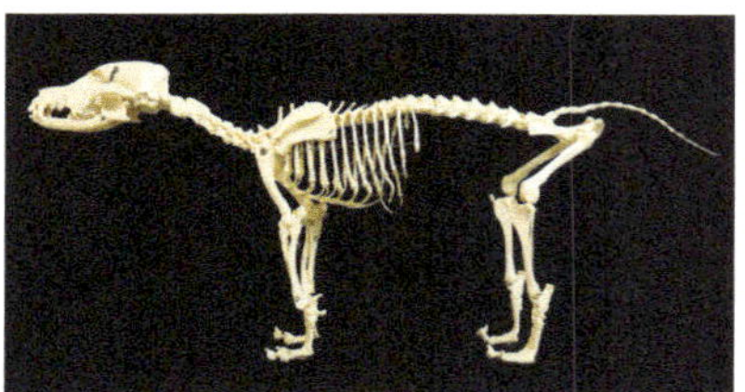

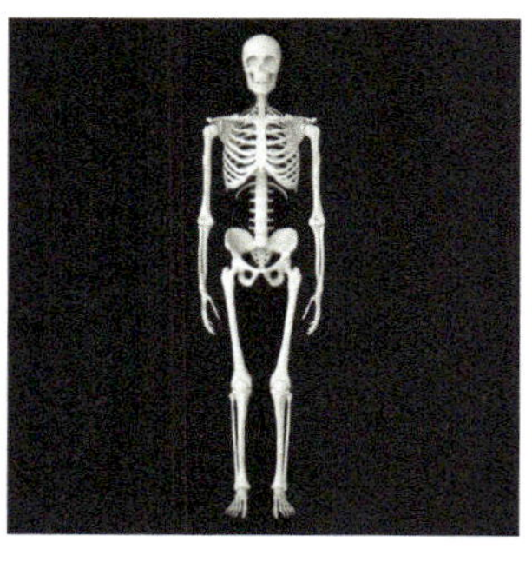

Point to the skeleton of the dog, fish, bird, snake, turtle, and human.

An **invertebrate** is an animal that has no backbone. It can have a soft body...

Or, it can have a hard, outer shell called an **exoskeleton** that protects its inner body.

Can you name two invertebrates with soft bodies? Can you name two invertebrates with exoskeletons?

Activity 1: Vertebrates and Invertebrates

1. What do you call an animal with a backbone inside its body?

2. Point to the animals that are vertebrates.

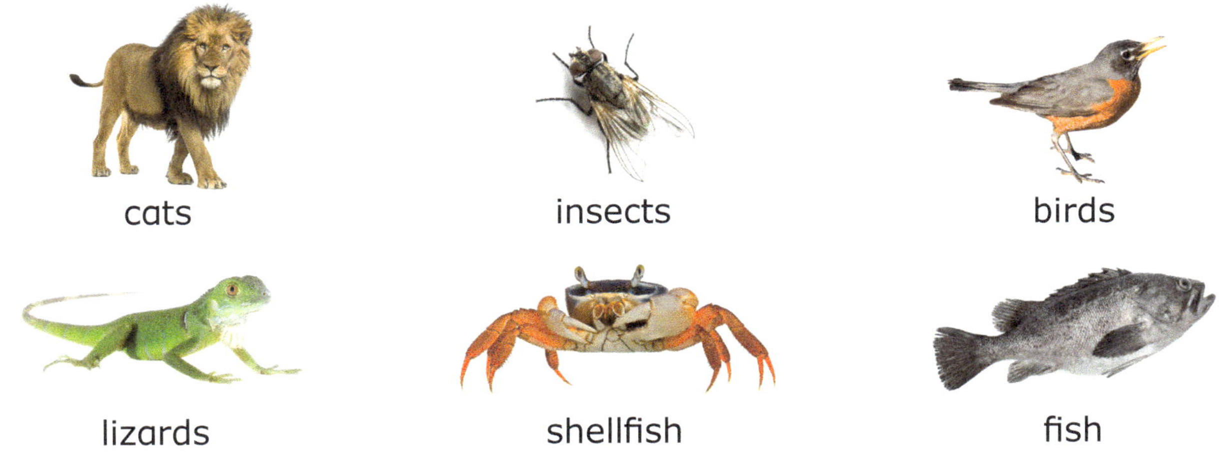

3. What do you call an animal that has no backbone?

4. Point to the invertebrates with an exoskeleton.

5. Point to the invertebrates without an exoskeleton.

Activity 2: Vertebrates and Invertebrates

Directions: Fill in the chart using **X** for yes and **–** for no as you solve the puzzle.

A ladybug, an octopus, and a sea turtle lay eggs. Find how many eggs each animal lays.

1. The invertebrate with 8 arms covered with suckers lays more eggs than the animal with a backbone inside of its a shell.

2. The animal with an exoskeleton has more legs than the vertebrate but lays fewer eggs.

Activity 3: Vertebrates and Invertebrates

Directions: Listen to the clues and match them to the animal they describe.

snail

tortoise

shrimp

centipede

elephant

rhinoceros

1. I hatch with my shell and it grows with me. My eyes are on the ends of my antenna. I am an invertebrate.

2. I have more than 10 legs. My exoskeleton is made of many segments. I can be found in moist soil.

3. I cover my skin in mud to cool off and avoid getting a sunburn. I am a vertebrate with a large backbone. I do not have horns on top of my head, but I do have tusks made of bone which help me to defend myself.

Activity 4: Vertebrates and Invertebrates

Directions: Listen to the clues and match them to the animal they describe. Then decide if the animal is a vertebrate or an invertebrate.

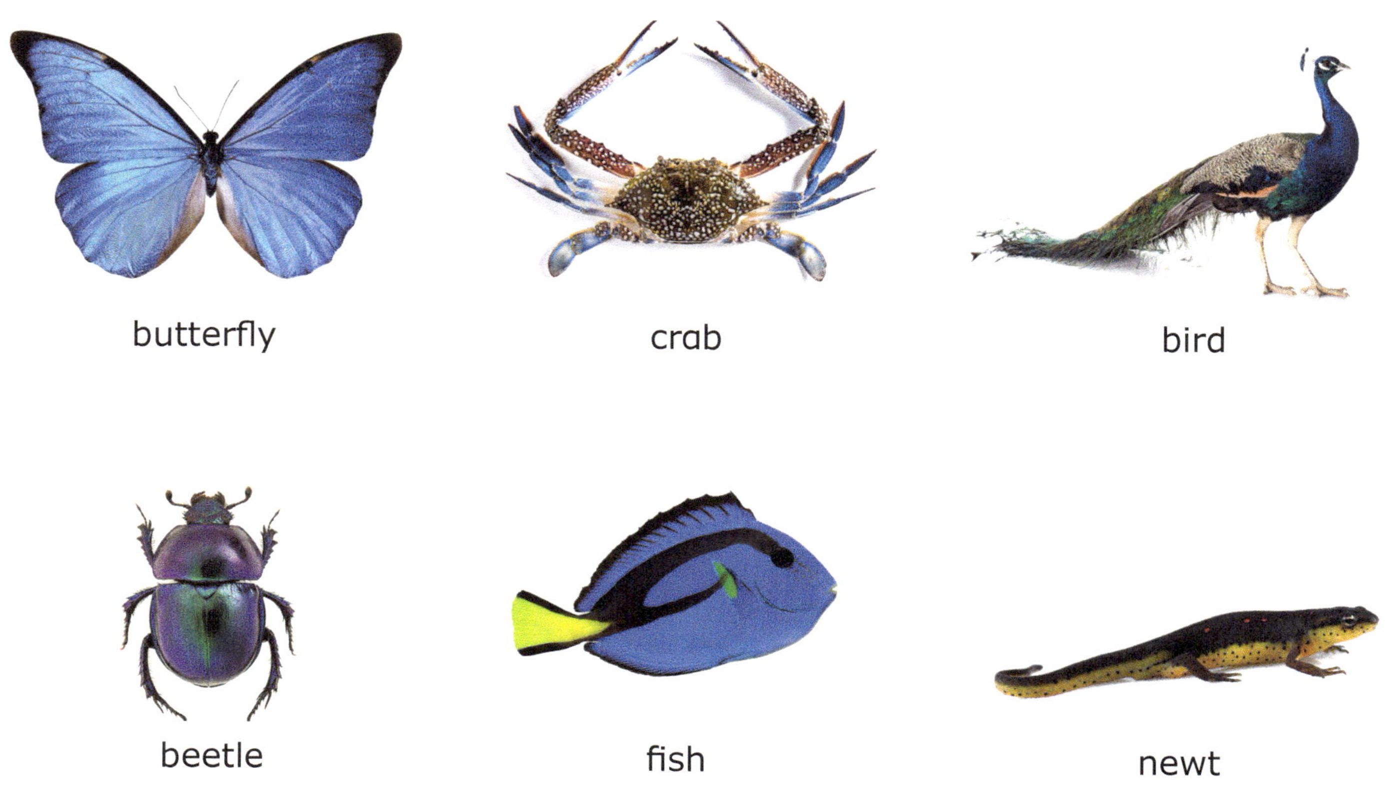

1. exoskeleton, 3 body segments, 6 legs, hidden wings

2. lives in water, soft skin, long flexible tail

3. wings, long tail, 2 legs

4. no tail, lives in water, crawls sideways, exoskeleton

Activity 5: Vertebrates and Invertebrates

Directions: Fill in the chart using **X** for yes and **–** for no as you solve the puzzle.

A tenrec, a porcupine fish, and a sea urchin all use spikes to defend themselves against predators. Find which food each animal eats.

1. The vertebrate with quills made of hair has clawed feet for digging up its prey.

2. The invertebrate without a brain, heart, or tail eats plankton that is scraped off rocks.

Activity 6: Vertebrates and Invertebrates

Directions: Listen to the clues and match them to the animal they describe.

sea star

squirrel

cardinal

butterfly

hornet

snake

1. Instead of bones, I have an exoskeleton to protect me from predators. I have an eye on the end of each of my 5 arms. I live in the ocean.

2. My wings are covered in scales and hairs. You can see my round, black, breathing holes along my exoskeleton. I have 6 long legs and do not sting.

3. I can climb trees. I make a chirping sound. My vertebrae end where my bushy tail begins.

Activity 7: Vertebrates and Invertebrates

Directions: Listen to the clues and match them to the animal they describe. Then decide if the animal is a vertebrate or an invertebrate.

octopus

parrot

red panda

agama

anemone

ladybug

1. soft body, no exoskeleton, suckers on all 8 legs

2. long, thin body with bones, body covered with scales

3. a slow-moving ocean animal without an exoskeleton, more than 10 tentacles

4. land animal, large beak, back bone, wings, two legs

Interesting Animals in This Lesson

radiated tortoise

These land animals are found on the tropical island of Madagascar. Their name comes from the yellow stripes that "radiate" down their shell, like the sun's rays. They spend their days grazing on grasses, fruits, and cacti. They have long lives and can live to be about as old as great-grandparents!

corn snake

These snakes can be found in the woods and meadows of the eastern U.S. Although they look similar to a more dangerous snake, corn snakes are not **venomous** (they don't inject poison when they bite). They catch their prey by wrapping around and squeezing it. They are good at hiding and like to slither through underground tunnels.

ladybug

Ladybugs (or lady beetles) can be red, orange, yellow, pink, blue, or grey! They can even have different numbers of spots. Their different colors are to warn predators that they taste bad and are toxic. People like ladybugs because they help in gardens by eating other bugs that hurt plants.

European hornet

This type of large wasp is most likely to attack and sting you if you are within 6 feet of their nest which looks like a brown paper ball. They eat sugar from fruits and other insects (especially honey). Only the 1 queen is allowed to lay eggs which they keep safe inside their nest.

blue tang

These fish live in coral reefs in the ocean and clean algae off the coral, sea turtles, and other fish. By cleaning other animals, the tang helps them to stay healthy. Some tangs live in groups called schools, and others swim alone. They protect themselves with sharp spines along their backs.

Northern cardinal

Male cardinals are bright red, but the females' brown color helps them to blend in with the tangled shrubs where they build their nests. They eat seeds, fruits, and insects. After their eggs hatch, both parents feed the chicks by giving them partly eaten food.

Review: Vertebrates and Invertebrates

Directions: Use a word from the choice box to describe each group.

Choice Box

vertebrates
exoskeleton
animals
invertebrates
no exoskeleton

1. ______________________

2. ______________________

3. ______________________

4. ______________________

5. ______________________

Research Question:

What is the largest invertebrate in the world?

Cold Blooded and Warm Blooded Animals

Some animals cannot warm or cool their bodies on their own. Animals who need the surrounding sun, air, or water to heat and cool their body temperature are called **cold blooded**. All invertebrates are cold blooded. A few vertebrates are also cold blooded: fish, **reptiles** (lizards, snakes, crocodiles, turtles, tortoises) and **amphibians** (frogs, toads, salamanders, newts). Here are some cold blooded animals:

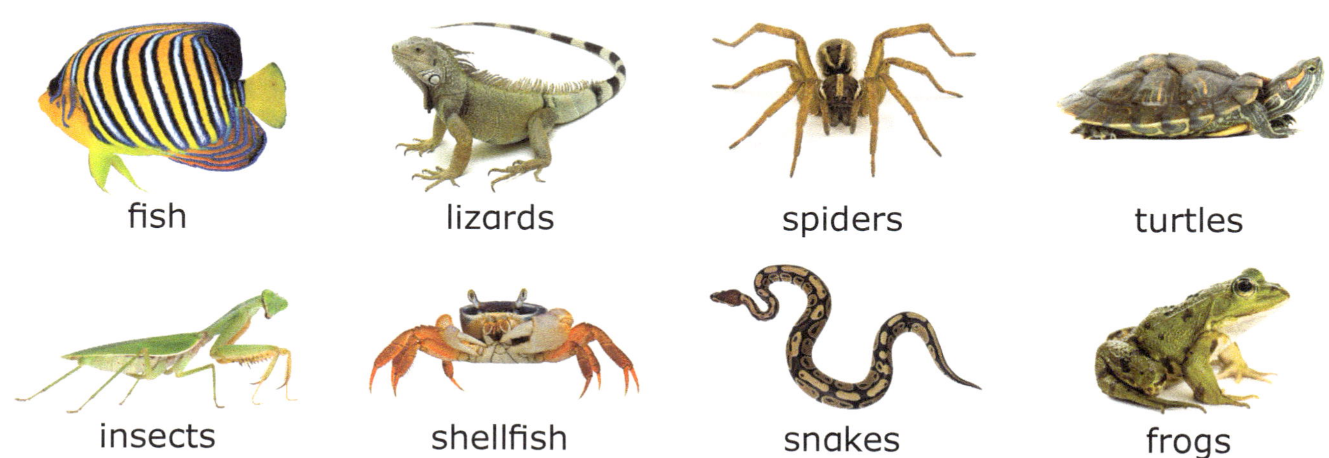

fish lizards spiders turtles

insects shellfish snakes frogs

Humans and other animals that maintain their own body temperature, even if it's hot or cold in their environment, are called **warm blooded**. All warm blooded animals have feathers or hair and four limbs. Their limbs are legs, arms, flippers, fins, or wings. Here are some warm blooded animals:

monkeys rodents birds

cats and dogs farm animals whales, dolphins, seals

Activity 1: Cold Blooded and Warm Blooded Animals

1. What do you call an animal that needs the sun, surrounding air, land, or water to heat and cool their body temperature?

2. All ______________________ are cold blooded. A few vertebrates are also cold blooded: fish, reptiles (lizards, snakes, crocodiles, turtles, tortoises) and amphibians (frogs, toads, salamanders, and newts).

3. Point to the animals that are cold blooded.

4. What do you call an animal that maintains its own temperature?

____

Remember, all warm blooded animals have feathers or hair and four limbs. Their limbs are legs, arms, flippers, fins, or wings.

5. Point to all animals with hair or feathers.

Activity 2: Cold Blooded and Warm Blooded Animals

Directions: Fill in the chart using **X** for yes and **–** for no as you solve the puzzle.

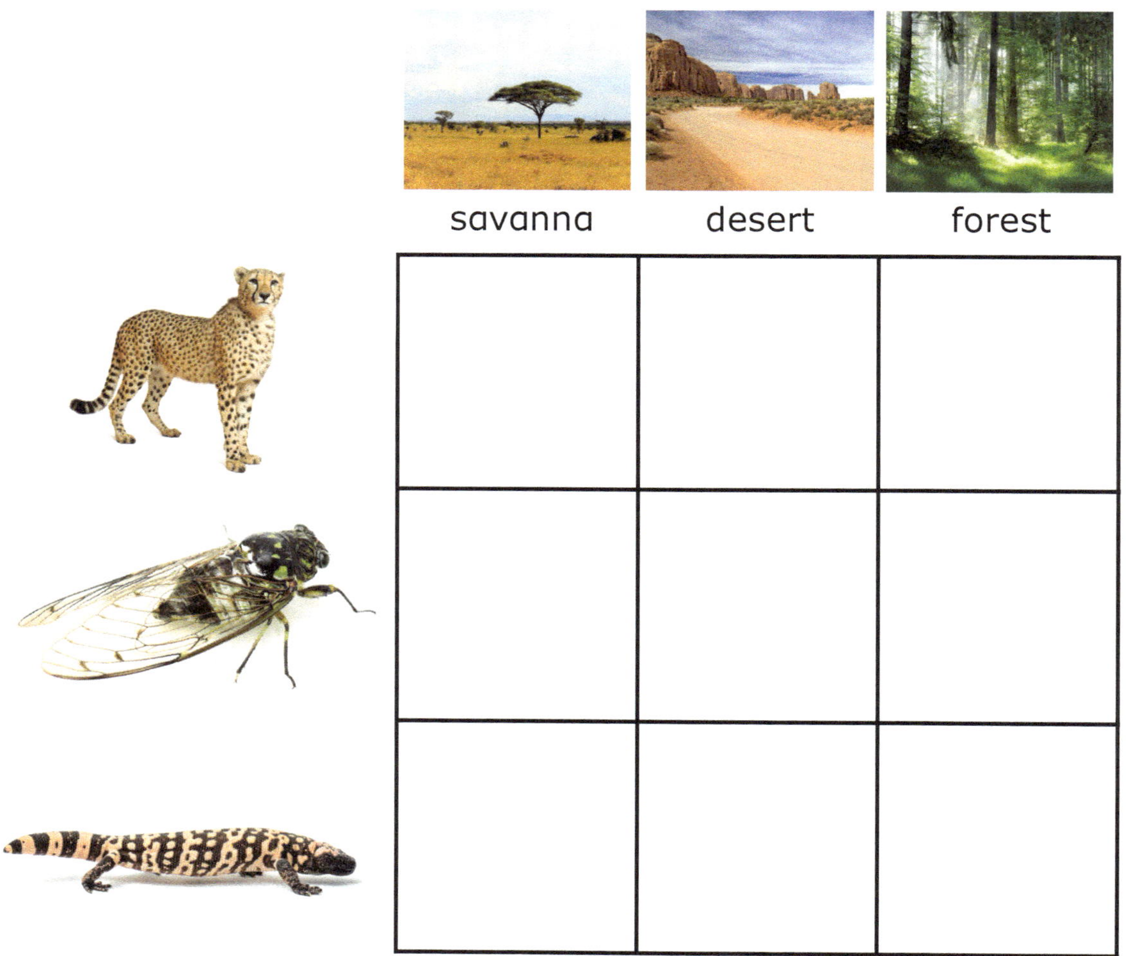

A cheetah, a cicada, and a Gila monster live in different **habitats**. Find where each animal lives.

1. The warm blooded vertebrate with fur that can run the fastest does not live in a forest.

2. The scaly, cold blooded vertebrate lives where it rains the least and the fewest plants grow.

Activity 3: Cold Blooded and Warm Blooded Animals

Directions: Listen to the clues and match them to the animal they describe.

ring-tailed lemur

tortoise

stingray

plecostomus

beetle

hawk

1. I am cold blooded and breathe underwater with gills. My spots help me to hide in my habitat. My long, thin tail helps me defend myself. My mouth is on my belly so I can eat off the bottom of the ocean.

2. I breathe air with lungs. I am cold blooded and sunbathe to keep warm. My backbone is attached to my shell.

3. My striped tail has two colors. I am a warm blooded vertebrate. I use special claws on my toes to brush my hair.

Activity 4: Cold Blooded and Warm Blooded Animals

Directions: Listen to the clues and match them to the animal they describe. Then decide if the animal is warm blooded or cold blooded.

praying mantis

owl

penguin

tarantula

toad

weasel

1. wings, webbed feet for swimming

2. hair, exoskeleton, 8 legs

3. land animal, vertebrate, fur

4. vertebrate, 4 legs, no hair

Activity 5: Cold Blooded and Warm Blooded Animals

Directions: Fill in the chart using **X** for yes and **–** for no as you solve the puzzle.

	2	4	5
(chameleon)			
(frog)			
(ostrich)			

A chameleon, a frog, and an ostrich have different types of feet. Find how many toes each animal has per foot.

1. The soft-skinned invertebrate with sticky feet has more toes than the large, warm blooded vertebrate.

2. The cold blooded vertebrate that changes colors to hide from predators has 3 toes on one side of its foot, 2 on the other side.

Activity 6: Cold Blooded and Warm Blooded Animals

Directions: Listen to the clues and match them to the animal they describe.

parrot

monkey

butterfly

ribbon eel

dragon sea-slug

pit viper

1. I am a short invertebrate with a soft body. My patterned blue and white body helps to hide me from predators. I'm cold blooded, so I use the water to control my body temperature.

2. I have a long, slender body with more ribs than you can count on your fingers and toes. I live on land and warm myself in the sunshine. The scales on my belly help me to slither without legs.

3. I eat the nectar from flowers and fruits. I am cold blooded so I spread my spotted wings in the sunshine to get warm.

Activity 7: Cold Blooded and Warm Blooded Animals

Directions: Listen to the clues and match them to the animal they describe. Then decide if the animal is warm blooded or cold blooded.

whale

scorpion

spider

bluebird

mouse

toad

1. long tail, pups drink milk, burrows underground

2. bumpy, hairless skin, vertebrate, long sticky toes

3. barbed tail, claws, exoskeleton

4. no toes, large animal, wide tail, calf drinks milk

Interesting Animals in This Lesson

humpback whale

Adult humpback whales can grow to be about the size of a school bus. Even though they are huge, they eat tiny shrimp called krill. Instead of chewing with teeth, they filter food through baleen which is similar to the bristles on a hairbrush. Calves stay with their mothers for about a year and drink milk.

ribbon eel

This sneaky fish hides in caves, crevices, or sand in lagoons and reefs of the ocean. It pokes its head out and uses its nose to lure small fish, shrimp, and crabs. When it's not eating, the eel opens and closes its mouth to help water flow through its gills so that it can breathe.

blue-and-yellow macaw

This large, tropical bird can grow to be about 3 feet long. In the wild it lives in a flock with about 100 other parrots. Macaws are talkative and can mimic human speech. They can also screech and blush if they are excited. Their strong, sharp beaks are used to crack open nuts.

wolf spider

This spider's 8 eyes give it excellent eyesight, so it does not need to use a web to catch its prey and sense the vibrations. Instead, it jumps onto its prey and injects venom. Mother wolf spiders carry their babies on their backs until the spiderlings are big enough to fend for themselves.

mandrill

Mandrills are the largest monkey. Most of their day is spent foraging for plants to eat on the rainforest floor. Females live in a huge horde that can have hundreds of family members. Males live on their own in the forest after they are about 6 years old.

knobbed whelk

A snail's body is attached to its shell and the shell grows with the snail. A sea snail has some of the strongest teeth in the Animal Kingdom. The radula, which is like a tongue with teeth, is used to scrape and cut a hole into the shell of its prey. Whelks live in the ocean and eat other shellfish and clams.

Review: Cold Blooded and Warm Blooded Animals

Directions: Use a word from the choice box to describe each group.

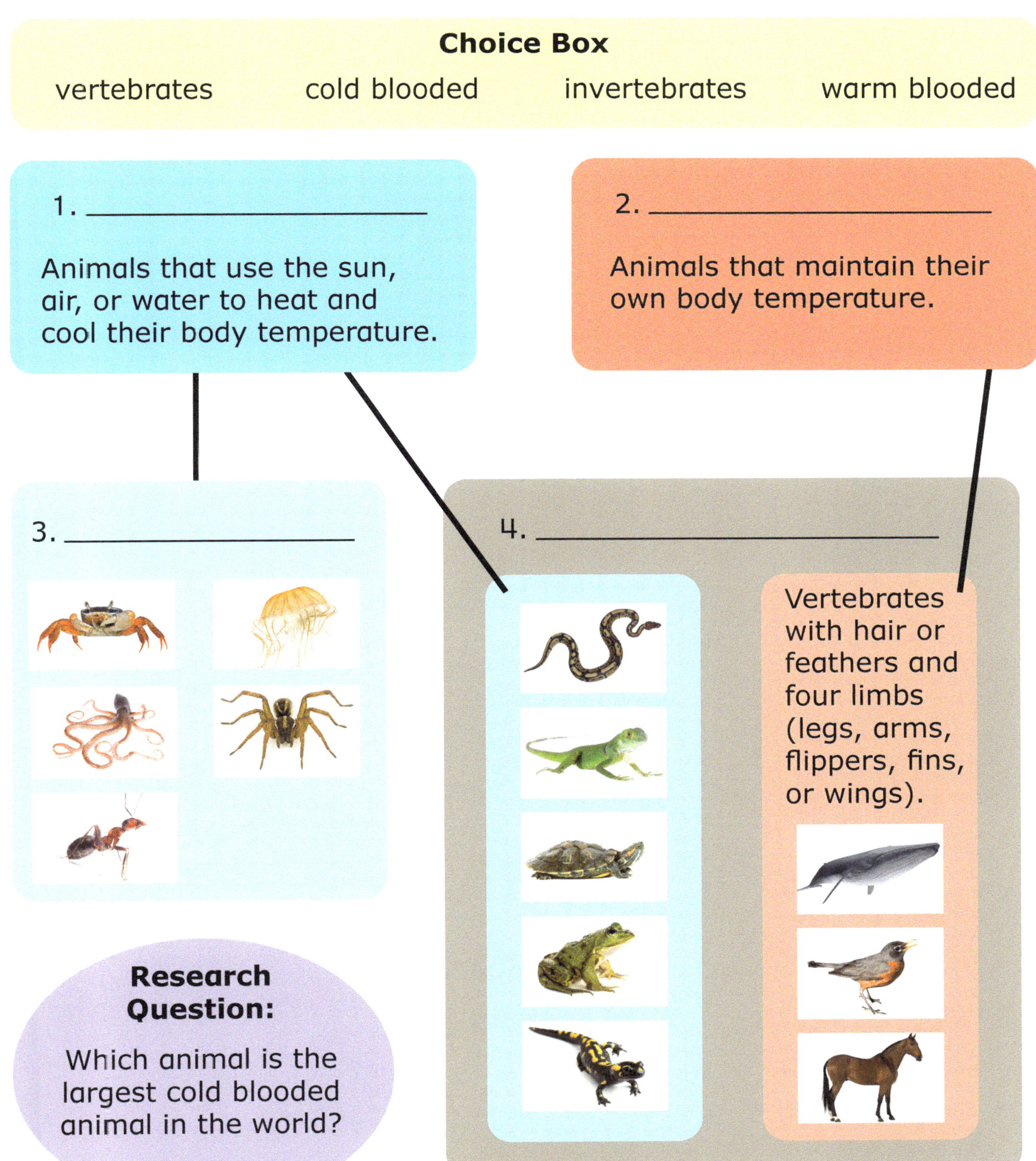

Mammals and Reptiles

Mammals are warm blooded vertebrates with hair. Feel the top of your head. Feel your eyebrows. Look at your arms and legs. Your skin is covered in hair! All mammals have hair, so you are a mammal!

Mammal hair helps them maintain body temperature, hide in their environment, and defend themselves. All mammals have hair, but hair can look and feel very different from your own. Here are some samples:

polar bear fur

rodent whiskers

porcupine quills

What can you observe about these animals' hairs and their functions?

Reptiles are cold blooded vertebrates that have bodies covered in scales. Scales help reptiles to move, defend themselves, retain water, and hide in their environment. Here are some samples:

lizards

crocodiles

turtles

snakes

tortoises

lizard underbelly

How do you think the reptiles scales help each reptile?

Activity 1: Mammals and Reptiles

1. Point to each animal and then explain how you know if it is a mammal or reptile.

2. Point to each animal and then explain how you know if it is warm blooded or cold blooded.

Activity 2: Mammals and Reptiles

Directions: Fill in the chart using **X** for yes and **–** for no as you solve the puzzle.

A koala, turtle, and a banded skink lizard all live in different habitats. Find where each animal lives.

1. The reptile with a long, scaley tail helps it to store water because it lives where there is lots of sand and very little water.

2. The mammal spends most of its life climbing from tree to tree eating leaves and branches.

Activity 3: Mammals and Reptiles

Directions: Listen to the clues and match them to the animal they describe.

hedgehog

river otter

garter snake

alligator

bottle-nose dolphin

pig-nosed turtle

1. I use the sun to warm my blood. The scales on my belly help me to move along the ground and climb trees. I do not have ears or legs. Mammal or Reptile? Which animal am I?

2. My long tail helps me to balance. I have webbed feet that make me a good swimmer. My fur helps me to stay warm even when I am wet. Mammal or Reptile? Which animal am I?

3. I have 4 short legs. I dig in the grass for worms to eat. I am a warm blooded vertebrate with spikey quills. Mammal or Reptile? Which animal am I?

Activity 4: Mammals and Reptiles

Directions: Listen to the clues and match them to the animal they describe. Then decide if the animal is a mammal or a reptile.

green anole

narwhal

green tree python

moose

box turtle

elephant seal

1. good climber, scales, 4 legs

2. cold blooded, slow moving, slither

3. water animal, whiskers, long tusk

4. land animal, warm blooded, hairy antlers

Activity 5: Mammals and Reptiles

Directions: Fill in the chart using **X** for yes and **–** for no as you solve the puzzle.

A snow leopard, a chameleon, and a giraffe live in different environments. Find each animal's habitat.

1. The cold blooded reptile lives in a warm, wet environment with lots of trees to climb.

2. The warm blooded animal with the shorter backbone has thick fur to keep it warm in a habitat that has frost year round.

Activity 6: Mammals and Reptiles

Directions: Listen to the clues and match them to the animal they describe.

flying squirrel

fox bat

red fox

milk snake

tortoise

bearded dragon

1. I am warm blooded and come out at night to eat. I have sensitive hearing. You can see my bones through my hairy wings when I fly. Mammal or Reptile? Which animal am I?

2. I live in the hot desert. To make sure the sun doesn't overheat my blood, I spend time underground. I have 4 legs and a long tail. Some of my scales look like spikes. Mammal or Reptile? Which animal am I?

3. I'm a vertebrate with soft fur. I have sharp teeth and eat small animals. My baby kits drink milk. Mammal or Reptile? Which animal am I?

*Flying squirrels don't technically fly, they glide.

Activity 7: Mammals and Reptiles

Directions: Listen to the clues and match them to the animal they describe. Then decide if the animal is a mammal or a reptile.

echidna

beaver

humpback whale

sea turtle

gecko

viper

1. no legs, pointy scales, sharp venomous fangs

2. long snout for eating ants and worms, quills made of hair for defense

3. cold blooded, large shell made of scales, short tail, sharp beak

4. warm blooded, calf drinks milk, long fins for swimming

Interesting Animals in This Lesson

American alligator

An alligator only eats 1-3 times a week because it is cold blooded and does not use a lot of energy. It can run, swim, jump, or climb to catch prey in a swamp habitat. Alligator mothers take care of their young for about a year after they hatch from their eggs.

milk snake

This harmless snake can grow to be 2 feet to 6 feet long. Snakes outgrow their skin in a process called molting. They shed their skin several times a year as they grow. Snakes do not have ears. Instead they "hear" vibrations through their bellies on the ground.

box turtle

A box turtle's home range is relatively small, usually smaller than your house. It likes to live in the woods near water. If you see a turtle in the wild, do not pick it up and move it because it could get lost and not know how to return home. Box turtles can live to be 50 to 100 years old!

elephant seal

It has fins for feet and moves faster in water than on land. It spends less than 2 months on land and does not eat during that time. The other 10 months of the year, elephant seals hunt fish in the ocean continuously. They can hold their breath underwater for about an hour and a half. Adult males can weigh as much as a car!

beaver

Beavers live around fresh water such as streams and ponds. They use tree branches, rocks, and mud to build dams. The dams cause water to flood an area, which creates a beaver pond. Beavers build their lodges on an island in the middle of the deep pond so that predators cannot reach them.

flying squirrel

This squirrel has a built-in cape that helps it to glide from tree to tree. It can "fly" about 150 feet. Gliding helps it to escape predators such as owls and snakes. Gliding also helps this squirrel spend most of its time high up in trees without needing to walk on the ground.

Review: Mammals and Reptiles

Directions: Use the words from the choice box to fill in the blanks.

Choice Box

limbs cold warm scales hair

1. __________ blooded with __________ and four __________.

2. __________ blooded with bodies covered in __________.

Research Question:

Do whales have hair?

Fish and Amphibians

Before you were born, you were growing inside of your mother. Unlike you, fish and amphibians first grow in tiny eggs laid in water! Fish and amphibians are both cold blooded vertebrates.

Amphibians begin life in water, but eventually spend part of their life on land. To live on land, amphibians grow lungs and legs. Here are some amphibians:

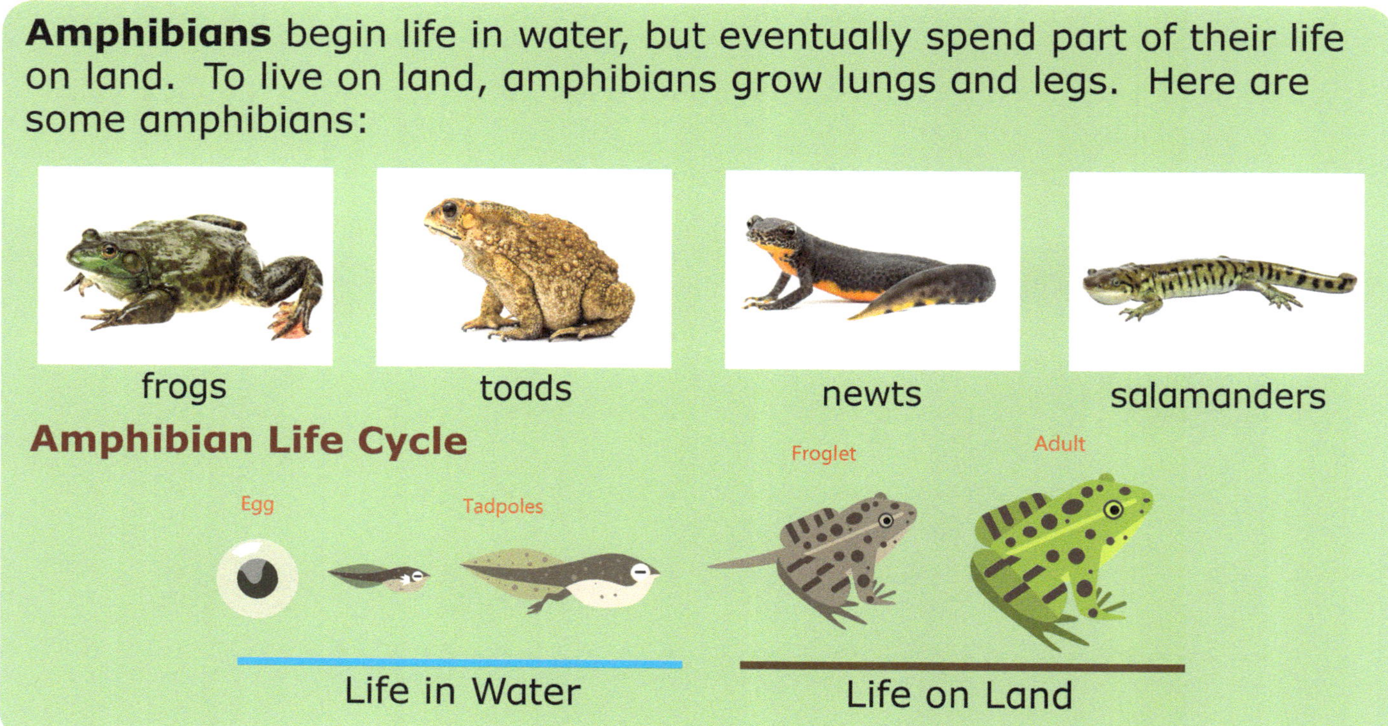

Fish spend their entire lives in water. They use fins to swim and gills to breathe. Here are some examples of fish:

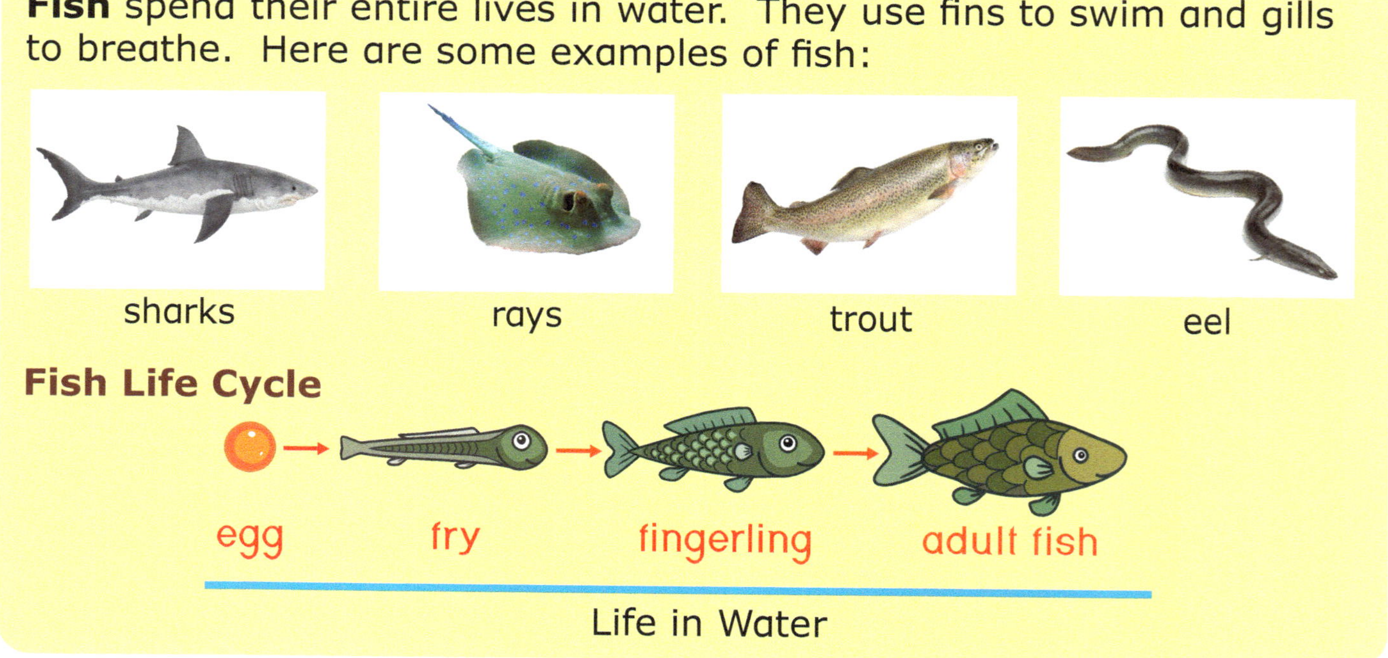

How are amphibians like fish? How are they different from fish as adults?

Activity 1: Fish and Amphibians

Directions: Draw a line from each item in the choice box to the correct group of animals it belongs to.

Choice Box

- born and live in water
- born in water, but live on land
- vertebrate

1.

2.

Directions: Draw a line from each animal to its square below.

Choice Box

3.

egg

Life in Water

4.

egg

Life in Water

Life on Land

Activity 2: Fish and Amphibians

Directions: Fill in the chart using **X** for yes and **–** for no as you solve the puzzle.

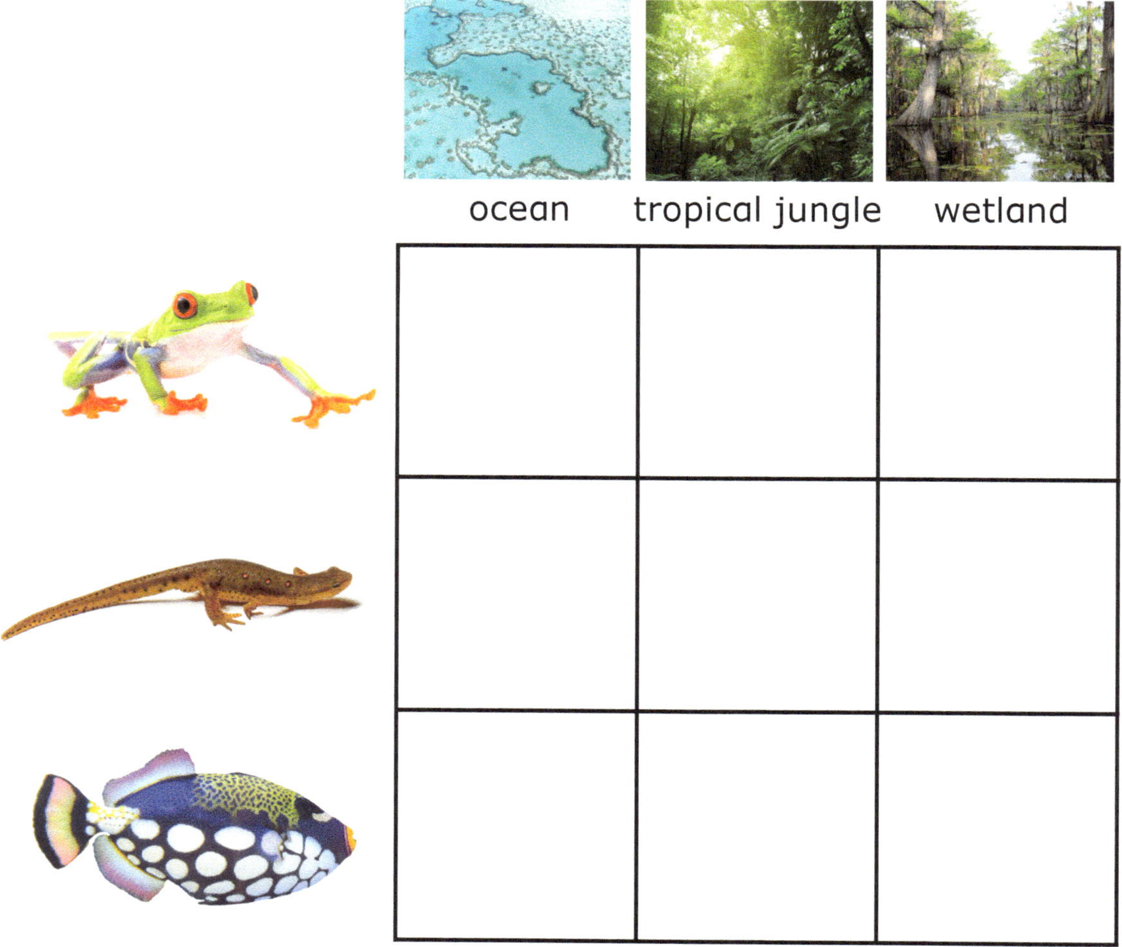

A red-eyed tree frog, a red-spotted newt, and a clown triggerfish live in different environments. Find each animal's habitat.

1. The amphibian that keeps its long tail as an adult can climb trees, but spends most of its time in water.

2. The vertebrate that breathes oxygen through gills its entire life never leaves the ocean.

Activity 3: Fish and Amphibians

Directions: Listen to the clues and match them to the animal they describe.

newt

salamander

toad

clown fish

mandarin fish

eel

1. As an adult, I have lungs to breathe air. I have 4 legs and can walk on land. My body shape is round and I haven't had a tail since I was young. Amphibian or Fish? Which animal am I?

2. I live my entire life in the water, so I use my gills to breathe. My body shape is long and narrow. You can barely see my tiny fins and sharp teeth. Amphibian or Fish? Which animal am I?

3. My long tail helps me to be a good swimmer. The spots on my skin help me to hide. As an adult, I have 4 legs that help me to walk on land where I spend a lot of time. Which animal am I?

Activity 4: Fish and Amphibians

Directions: Listen to the clues and match them to the animal they describe. Then decide if the animal is a fish or amphibian.

tomato frog

newt

fire salamander

hammerhead shark

stingray

rainbow trout

1. thin tail, spotted pattern, flat and round
2. adult walks on land and has no tail, round shaped body
3. adult spends most time on land, long tail, 4 legs
4. gills, long tail, 7 large fins, many teeth

Activity 5: Fish and Amphibians

Directions: Fill in the chart using **X** for yes and **−** for no as you solve the puzzle.

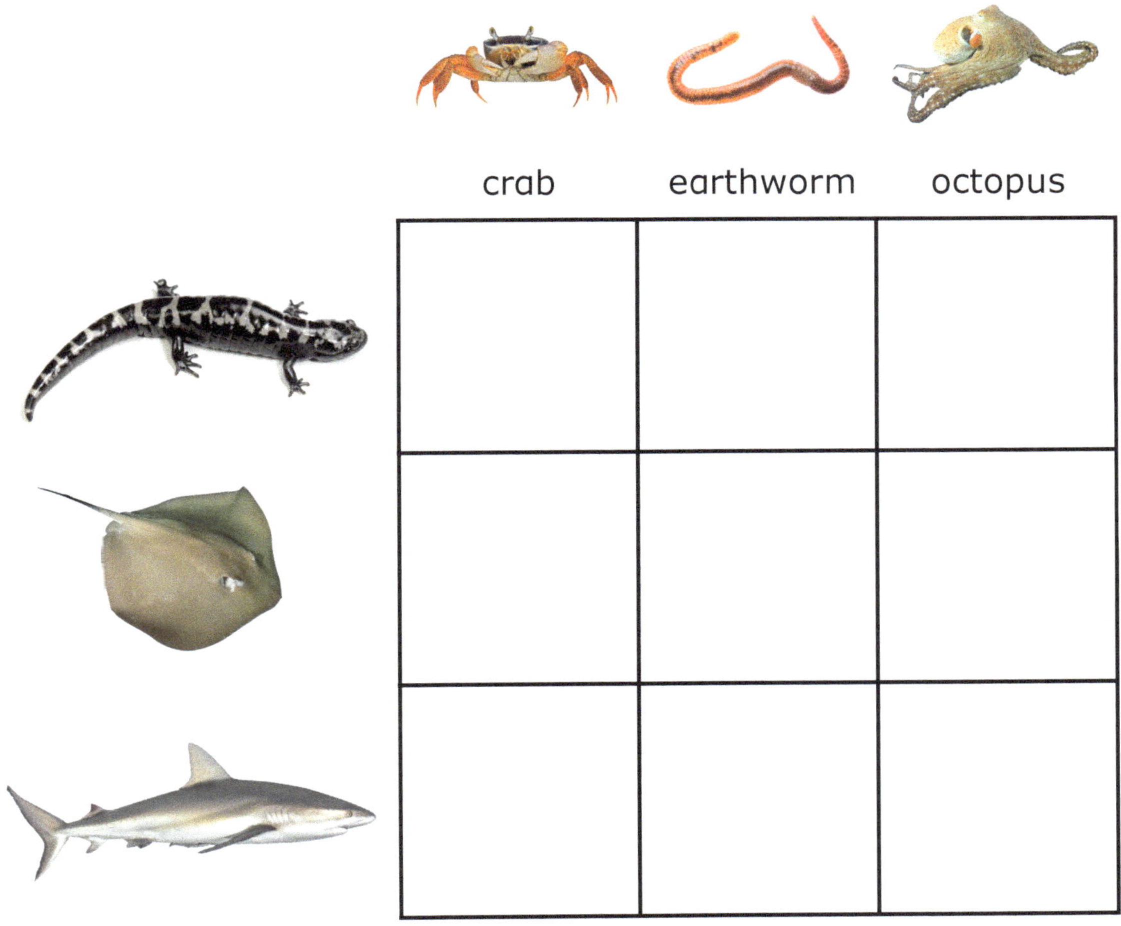

A fire salamander, a stingray, and a sandbar shark eat other animals. Find each animal's favorite food.

1. The animals that breathe through gills do not have legs to dig for the land invertebrate with no exoskeleton.

2. The vertebrate that is round and flat like a pancake hunts at night for the animal with the exoskeleton that walks on the ocean floor.

Activity 6: Fish and Amphibians

Directions: Listen to the clues and match them to the animal they describe.

tadpole

froglet

frog

arowana

seahorse

striped marlin

1. My long tail curls around plant stems in the water to help me stay in one place. My gills let me breath underwater, and my fins help me to swim. Some people say my face looks like a mammal, which is how I got my name. Amphibian or Fish? Which animal am I?

2. When I'm young, I spend all my time swimming in the water breathing through my gills. I have a long, thin tail and no legs—yet. Amphibian or Fish? Which animal am I?

3. I spend my entire life in the water. My skin is covered in large scales. The large fins by my tail help me to balance. Amphibian or Fish? Which animal am I?

Activity 7: Fish and Amphibians

Directions: Listen to the clues and match them to the animal they describe. Then decide if the animal is a fish or amphibian.

salamander and eggs

newt larva*

newt

rainbow fish

sturgeon fry*

sturgeon

1. not an adult, external feathery looking gills above my head

2. adult, lungs, long worm-like tail

3. adult, scales, fins, mouth on the bottom of my head

4. gills, not an adult, will soon grow scales

*Larva and fry are developing young that have not reached adult shape and size.

Interesting Animals in This Lesson

red salamander

Even though they are cold blooded, red salamander eggs hatch in winter in the U.S. Rain during the winter means there are plenty of wet places for the females to lay eggs. In the summer there is more risk of drought. Red salamander eggs take 1 to 3 weeks to hatch.

red-eyed treefrog

It rests in green leaves and trees with its eyes closed, so predators have a hard time seeing it. But if the treefrog is startled, it opens its red eyes. The red color warns predators that it tastes bad. Since this treefrog is not poisonous, its eye color is its only defense against animals that want to eat it.

common newt

Newts have lungs and can breathe on land. But they can also absorb oxygen through their skin, so they can stay in fresh water such as ponds and streams without "coming up for air." On land, they use their sticky tongues to catch small bugs, worms, and snails. In water, they catch prey with their teeth.

sandbar shark

This shark got its name from often being seen in warm water close to the coast. Shark skin feels hard and scratchy like sandpaper. The skin is made of tough scales or "skin teeth." This tough skin protects the shark from other shark bites. It also helps the shark to swim faster.

rainbow trout

These fish are originally from the U.S. west of the Rocky Mountains, but have been introduced to rivers, lakes, and seas across the world. They eat small fish, eggs, bugs, and amphibians. Their skin feels slimy because it is covered in a layer of mucus (like snot!) that protects them from germs in the water.

blue-spotted stingray

Stingray teeth are called dental plates. It uses them to crush animals with hard shells such as crabs and shrimp that are walking on the ocean floor. Its gills are on their underside by the mouth. When it hides in the sand, the breathing hole behind its eye helps it to breathe.

Review: Fish and Amphibians

Directions: Use the words from the choice box to fill in the blanks.

Choice Box

fish	water	amphibians	land
vertebrates	cold	cold	vertebrates

1. ______________ are ______________ blooded ______________ that spend their entire life in ______________.

2. ______________ are ______________ blooded ______________ that begin life in water but live on ______________ as adults.

Thinker Question:

How do you know this developing animal is an amphibian and not a fish?

Research Question:

Why do fish and amphibians lay so many eggs?

Carnivore, Herbivore, and Omnivore

Think about your favorite foods. Do you like to eat plant foods like fruits, vegetables, and nuts? Do you eat meat like chicken, beef, and fish? Animals that eat plant foods and meat foods are called omnivores.

An **omnivore** is an animal that eats both plants and animals. Here are some examples:

humans

bluebirds

crabs

What advantage does an omnivore have over herbivores and carnivores?

A **carnivore** is an animal that only eats other animals (meat). Here are some examples:

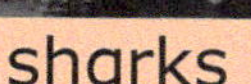
sharks

lions

crocodiles

What do all of these carnivores have in common?

An **herbivore** is an animal that only eats plants. Here are some examples:

butterflies

koalas

tortoises

How do these herbivores look different from carnivores?

Activity 1: Carnivore, Herbivore, and Omnivore

Directions: Look at the pictures and read the clue for each group. Then point to each animal and say if it is a carnivore, herbivore, or omnivore.

1. The chimpanzee eats animals and plants.

2. The bear eats more than plants.

3. The gorilla does not eat animals.

4. The wolf does not eat plants.

Activity 2: Carnivore, Herbivore, and Omnivore

Directions: Fill in the chart using **X** for yes and **–** for no as you solve the puzzle.

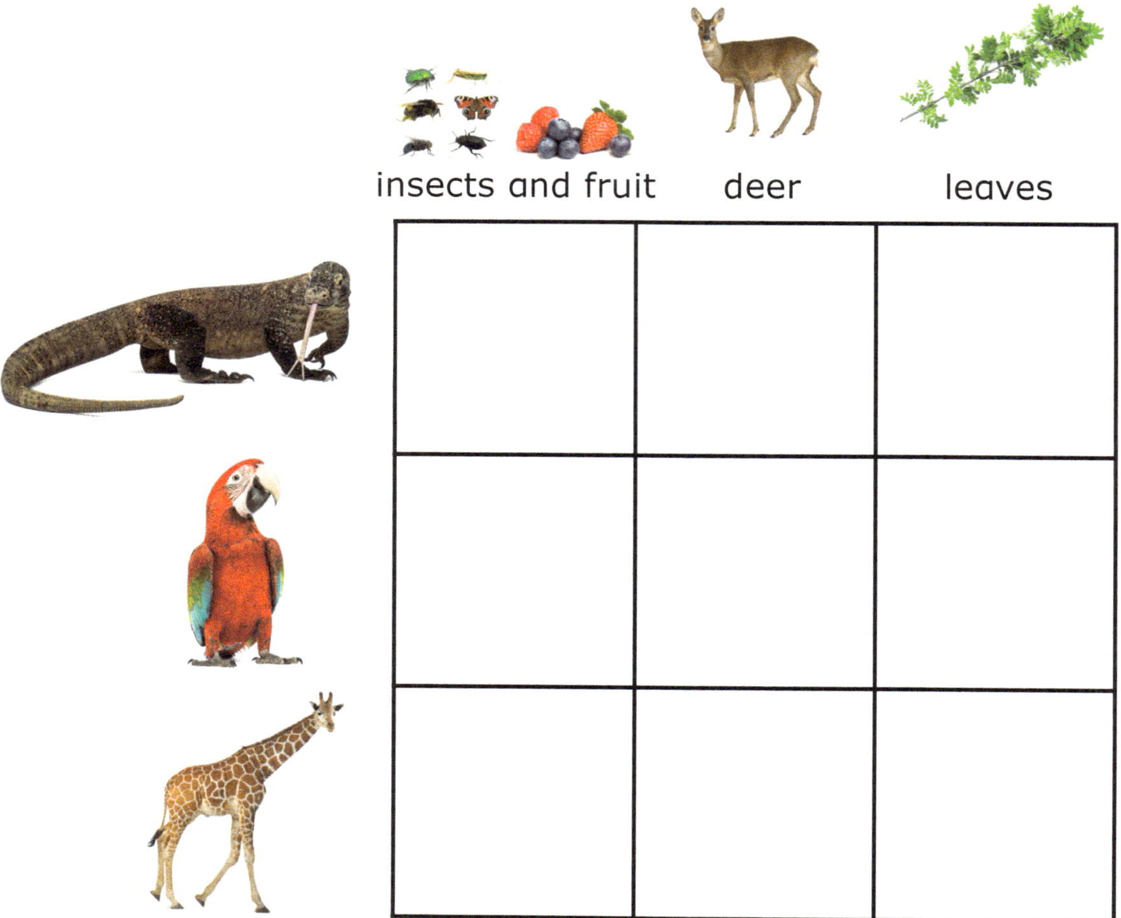

A Komodo dragon, a parrot, and a giraffe each have different favorite foods. Find what each animal likes to eat.

1. The herbivore that always walks on 4 furry legs does not prefer sweets.

2. The feathered animal sometimes eats food that can fly or crawl.

Activity 3: Carnivore, Herbivore, and Omnivore

Directions: Listen to the clues and match them to the animal they describe.

Komodo dragon

millipede

dragonfly

elephant seal

jelly fish

pipefish

1. I am an invertebrate with an exoskeleton. I live on land and am an omnivore. I do not have wings.

2. I have a long tail. My claws help me to dig a burrow where I lay my eggs. I am a carnivore with a forked tongue that helps me to smell the large prey I will hunt and eat.

3. I live in the water and breathe with gills. I am a carnivore with a long body and pointy nose that helps me to eat small shrimps and plankton.

Activity 4: Carnivore, Herbivore, and Omnivore

Directions: Listen to the clues and match them to the animal they describe.

scorpion

pit viper

river otter

three-toed sloth

tarantula

sea star

1. hairy legs, exoskeleton, carnivore, 8 eyes, no tail

2. scales, vertebrate, long tongue, carnivore

3. slow moving, ocean animal, cold blooded, omnivore

4. mammal, hooked claws, herbivore, tree hanger

Activity 5: Carnivore, Herbivore, and Omnivore

Directions: Fill in the chart using **X** for yes and **–** for no as you solve the puzzle.

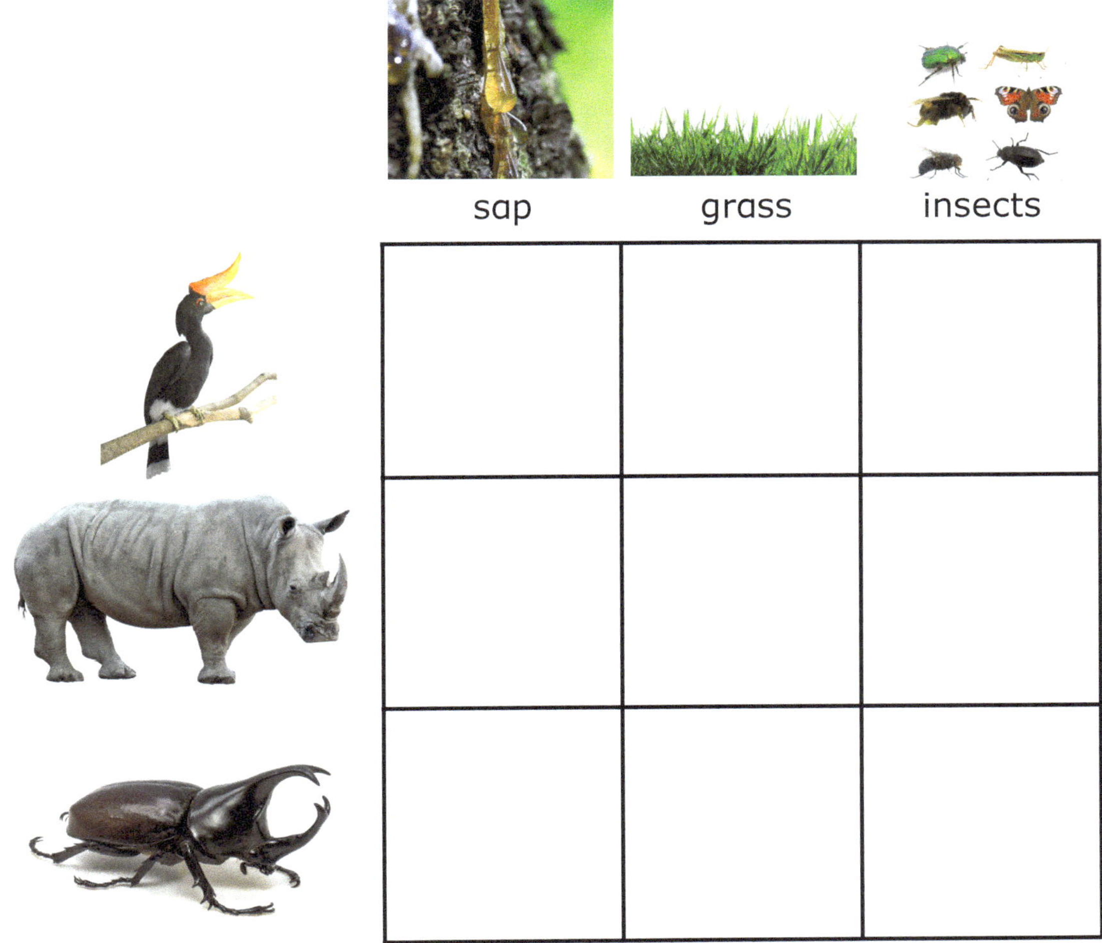

A crowned hornbill bird, a rhinoceros, and a rhino beetle eat different foods. Find each animal's diet.

1. The animal with the most legs is an herbivore and does not eat other animals like the feathered bird with talons.

2. The animal with an exoskeleton sucks its meal out of a tree, but the mammal chews its food.

Activity 6: Carnivore, Herbivore, and Omnivore

Directions: Listen to the clues and match them to the animal they describe.

sea urchin

dragonfly

starling

hummingbird

toad

siamese fighting fish

1. I am an omnivore with sticky feet that help me to climb on to surfaces. I can live longer than most other animals. Instead of bones, I have a spiky exoskeleton.

2. I have wings. I lay eggs. Although my beak is specially shaped like a straw to drink nectar from flowers, I am an omnivore that sometimes eats insects.

3. I am a reptile with more than 2 legs. I am a carnivore and blinking helps me to swallow my prey. I live near water but spend most of my time on land.

Activity 7: Carnivore, Herbivore, and Omnivore

Directions: Listen to the clues and match them to the animal they describe.

poison dart frog

ostrich

brown bear

ring-tailed lemur

lion

elephant

1. omnivore, mammal, grasping hands, striped tail

2. carnivore, long tail, fur covered paws

3. herbivore, fast runner, feathered wings

4. carnivore, soft skinned amphibian, sticky feet and tongue

Interesting Animals in This Lesson

brown bear

In the summer and fall, a brown bear eats about 85 pounds of food a day! (The average 6-year-old human weighs 50 pounds.) Bears will sample anything but most of their diet comes from plants. When they hunt, they prey on animals that are easy to catch. Or they eat animals that are already dead.

compass jellyfish

Jellyfish use their string-like tentacles to catch tiny plants and animals (called plankton and zooplankton). When it catches larger prey such as fish, its tentacles sting and kill the prey with venomous barbs. Then the ribbon-like oral arms bring the food to its mouth inside the "bell." A jellyfish does not poop, so it spits out food waste when it is done eating.

river otter

Whiskers on the river otter's face help it to hunt. These hairs sense motion in the air, water, and ground where an otter is searching for food. The vibrations caused by movement can tell the otter the size and location of its prey. River otters eat fish, clams, amphibians, snakes, small mammals- basically any type of small animal it can catch!

elephant

An elephant uses its trunk as a nose, arm, and water sprinkler. Its trunk is used to suck up water and spray on its back to keep cool. Elephants are the heaviest land animal, but they only eat plants! They are always dining on leaves, bark, and roots.

Siamese fighting fish

This fish is smaller than the palm of your hand. Its mouth points upward so that it can eat tiny things off the surface of the water such as zooplankton, insect larva, and small water animals. This fish has special gills to breathe oxygen through water and through gulping air with its mouth.

Emperor scorpion

Scorpions are nocturnal (they come out at night). They have poor eyesight and rely more on the hairs on their legs to sense prey moving near them. Young scorpions use their stinging tail to inject venom to poison their prey. Adult scorpions use their strong claws to crush their prey.

Review: Carnivore, Herbivore, and Omnivore

Directions: Draw a line connecting each group of animals to the food group they eat.

meat

meat and plants

plants

carnivore

herbivore

omnivore

Thinker Question:

Can an omnivore eat a carnivore? Explain how this could or could not happen.

Research Question:

Which animal is the largest omnivore in the world?

Types of Birds

Birds are warm blooded vertebrates that have feathers, wings, beaks, and hard-shelled eggs. Here are 3 main types of birds:

Songbirds are usually small, perching birds that are known for their vocalizing which they use to attract mates and establish their territories. They typically have small beaks for eating nuts, seeds, fruits, insects, and worms. Here are some examples:

robins

sparrows

house finches

Water birds are usually medium to large sized birds with webbed feet and beaks specially shaped to scoop fish, shrimp, and crabs out of the water. They tend to lay their eggs in nests built in or near water. Here are some examples:

swans

puffins

seagulls

Birds of prey are hunters of small animals. They have sharp talons and a pointed beak to tear meat. Here are some examples:

vultures

eagles

hawks

How are songbirds different from water birds and birds of prey?

Activity 1: Types of Birds

1. Point to each bird and then say if it is a song bird, water bird, or bird of prey.

2. Point to each picture and then explain if this is a song bird, water bird, or bird of prey.

Research Questions:

What is the largest bird in the world?
Name three types of birds that can't fly.

Activity 2: Types of Birds

Directions: Fill in the chart using **X** for yes and **▬** for no as you solve the puzzle.

A barn owl, a cardinal, and a penguin have different diets. Find what each animal eats.

1. The songbird with the smallest beak eats the smallest food.

2. The water bird hunts for its prey by swimming in the ocean.

Activity 3: Types of Birds

Directions: Listen to the clues and match them to the animal they describe.

buzzard

mallard duck

cardinal

penguin

robin

bald eagle

1. I am a songbird and omnivore that spends most of my time on the ground looking for worms. My song sounds like I am singing, "cheerily, cheer up, cheer up, cheerily, cheer up!" My head and breast have different colors.

2. I am a water bird. My chicks are able to swim immediately after hatching. I am an omnivore. People often feed me bread when they see me at the parks but it's not good for me. Peas, corn, or small pieces of meat are much healthier treats for me.

3. I am a bird of prey that likes to eat small mammals. Some people say my call sounds like a cat's meow. When I'm an adult, all my feathers are brown.

Activity 4: Types of Birds

Directions: Listen to the clues and match them to the animal they describe. Then decide if the bird is a songbird, water bird, or a bird of prey.

great horned owl

stork

thrush

goose

osprey

warbler

1. brown and white feathers, omnivore, speckled belly

2. carnivore, sharp talons, sharp beak, usually sleeps during the day

3. large bird, omnivore, webbed feet for swimming, long neck, short beak

4. long legs, long beak to catch fish, webbed feet

Activity 5: Types of Birds

Directions: Fill in the chart using **X** for yes and **–** for no as you solve the puzzle.

A goose, a sparrow, and a marsh harrier have different life expectancies. Find how many years each animal can live.

1. The smallest bird with the smallest beak lives the fewest years but has the prettiest song.

2. The bird of prey does not live as long as the water bird.

Activity 6: Types of Birds

Directions: Listen to the clues and match them to the animal they describe.

phoebe

goose

duck

falcon

tanager

turkey vulture

1. I am a carnivore that eats the meat of dead animals. My face is bare so that I don't have to clean it after I eat. I have dark feathers and sharp talons and beak. Which type of bird am I?

2. My short, thin beak is good for catching flying insects and pecking at seeds. If you see me perched on a branch, you'll notice I flick my tail while I sing. My whole body is different shades of gray. Which type of bird am I?

3. My webbed feet help me to paddle in the water. Some people say my call sounds like a "honk!" My neck is longer than the other water bird's. Which type of bird am I?

Activity 7: Types of Birds

Directions: Listen to the clues and match them to the animal they describe. Then decide if the bird is a songbird, water bird, or a bird of prey.

pelican

kingbird

seagull

great horned owl

finch

kestrel

1. omnivore with 3 small toes on each foot for gripping, small, colorful head, short beak for picking up insects, worms, nuts, and berries; cheerful whistling song

2. small hunter of rodents and reptiles, pointed beak, sharp talons, black spots on red breast and back

3. black, white, and gray feathers, salt water habitat, short, sharp bill for ripping apart fish, will eat just about anything

4. wingspan longer than your dad is tall, webbed feet, bill longer than your foot

Interesting Animals in This Lesson

puffin

A true water bird, puffins float around the sea for 8 months of the year. They can stay underwater for up to 2 minutes when they swim and dive for fish. In the late spring and summer, they return to the coast where they were born. They choose the same mate every year and lay only 1 egg per year.

great horned owl

Owls cannot move their eyes, but they can turn their head all the way around. They can also hear even small sounds like mouse feet scratching on dried leaves far away. They hunt small mammals, reptiles, and amphibians. Their sharp talons and beak help them to rip apart their prey. Owls prefer to eat every day.

Couch's kingbird

Early in the morning the male kingbird will sing his song to alert other birds that this is his territory. His song also lets females know that he is in the area. Kingbirds eat flying insects. They perch on a tree branch near a meadow and watch for prey. They catch insects in the air or hover over them.

gentoo penguin

The gentoo is the fastest swimming penguin and can stay underwater for up to 7 minutes. They hunt for small fish and swallow their prey whole (and alive)! Because they don't chew their food, a penguin chooses fish that are swimming in the same direction so that they will fit in its beak.

osprey

It hunts for fish in rivers, lakes, and seas. Once it sees its prey, it drops feet-first into the water to grab fish with its sharp talons. Its outer toe is specially designed to help hold onto wriggling, slippery fish. Birds have no teeth, so an osprey rips apart its prey with its pointed beak.

garden warbler

This little songbird is a serious traveler. It spends its summers in Eurasia and flies south to Africa for the warmer winter. To fatten up for the long flight, it eats lots of figs and insects. In the spring, it mostly feeds insects and small invertebrates to its chicks to help them build muscle.

Review: Types of Birds

Directions: Circle each true description for each group of birds.

1.	2.	3.

bird of prey **or** song bird	bird of prey **or** water bird	bird of prey **or** song bird
vertebrate **or** invertebrate	vertebrate **or** invertebrate	vertebrate **or** invertebrate
warm blooded **or** cold blooded	warm blooded **or** cold blooded	warm blooded **or** cold blooded
small **or** large	small and large **or** small	small and large **or** large
webbed feet **or** no webbed feet	webbed feet **or** no webbed feet	webbed feet **or** no webbed feet
talons **or** no talons	talons **or** no talons	talons **or** no talons
carnivore **or** omnivore		carnivore **or** omnivore

Research Question:

Are all water birds carnivores?

Camouflage

Animals sometimes use their body coloring and shape to hide from other animals. This is called camouflage. Animals use camouflage to hide from **predators** (animals that are trying to catch and eat them). They also use camouflage to hide themselves from **prey** (animals they are hunting).

scorpion

polar bear

chipmunk

sea star

How do these animals' colors help them to hide themselves?

bird eggs

octopus

garter snake

plecostomus

How do these animals' patterns help them to hide themselves?

treehopper

stick bug

flounder

alligator

How do these animals' shapes help them to hide themselves?

Activity 1: Camouflage

Directions: Each group of camouflaged animals includes one predator and two animals that it preys on. Point to the predator and explain how each of its prey hides from it.

Activity 2: Camouflage

Directions: Listen to the clues and match them to the animal they describe.

frog duck frogfish

moth jaguar lizard

1. My pattern helps me to blend in with leaves and branches. I have dark spots. I am a mammal and a predator.

2. I am a cold-blooded vertebrate. My color and shape help me to hide in plain sight. My long body blends in with tree bark.

3. My color helps to disguise me when I rest. I am prey that is eaten by many animals. I am an invertebrate.

Activity 3: Camouflage

Directions: Listen to the clues and match them to the animal they describe.

rabbit

frog

beach wolf spider

owl

silky shark

sea turtle

1. predator, different color top and bottom, underwater, gills

2. prey, herbivore, 4 legs, warm blooded

3. prey, pattern disguised with algae, cold blooded, reptile

4. carnivore, pattern and color blend in, warm blooded

Activity 4: Camouflage

Directions: Listen to the clues and match them to the animal they describe.

arctic fox | deer | katydid leafbug

spider | sole | hump-nosed lizard

1. I am a predator with more than four legs. I use color to hide from my prey. I can change color depending on where I am. I do not have wings.

2. My color and shape help me to hide in trees and bushes. If I am still then maybe predators won't notice me. My exoskeleton looks like a leaf.

3. I am a predator that uses my body shape to hide before attacking my prey. I can bury myself with sand to help blend in with the ground. I am a cold blooded vertebrate.

Activity 5: Camouflage

Directions: Listen to the clues and match them to the animal they describe.

ibex | oakleaf butterfly | reef octopus

chipmunk | spider | woodcock

1. soft bodied invertebrate that can change shape and color; gills

2. prey, striped pattern, mammal

3. predator, looks like sticks on the ground, exoskeleton

4. pattern and color camouflage, warm blooded, long beak

Interesting Animals in This Lesson

ibex

An ibex is a wild mountain goat that climbs cliffs and eats vegetation along the way. Their hooves are like suction cups that help them grip steep mountain walls without falling off. Because they live in places that are hard to walk in, their main predators are eagles and vultures.

wood frog

Frogs have long, sticky tongues that they use to catch their food. The special teeth on the roof of their mouth help them to keep prey inside. When a frog is ready to swallow, it closes its eyes to help it push the food down its throat. Frogs eat things like slugs and bugs.

white-tailed deer

Deer are herbivores that spend time grazing in the forest. When it feels threatened or thinks there is danger, it raises its tail in warning so other deer can see the white part and know to be careful or to run away. People, wolves, bears, and coyotes are just a few predators that hunt deer.

arctic fox

Arctic fox fur changes color depending on the season. In the snowy winter months, the fox fur is all white. In the warm summer, the fox fur is grey or brown. It hunts all year so the fur color helps it to hide from prey (rodents, fish, and birds) and predators (wolves, birds of prey, and bears).

hump-nosed lizard

This lizard crawls through grass and vegetation during the day and rests in trees at night. To "scare" predators, it opens its mouth to show a bright red color inside. If that does not work, its only other defense is to run. Because so many larger animals want to eat it, its best option is to stay camouflaged.

oakleaf butterfly

When a butterfly lands on something to rest or eat, it does so with its wings closed together. If a bird tries to chase it, the butterfly will land on fallen leaves and be very still so that it becomes "invisible" to the predator. The oakleaf butterfly changes patterns and colors depending on the season.

Review: Camouflage

Directions: Fill in the chart using **X** for yes and **▬** for no as you solve the puzzle.

A cheetah, raccoon, and giraffe all use camouflage to hide. Find each animals favorite food.

1. I'm a predator and a carnivore known for my speed.

2. I'm not the tallest, but I am an ominvore.

Review Activity 1

Directions: Fill in the chart using **X** for yes and **–** for no as you solve the puzzle.

An crane, a giant tortoise, and a leopard grow to be different sizes. Find how tall each animal can grow.

1. The warm blooded animal with the fewest legs is taller than the carnivore with fur, but not as tall as the cold blooded reptile.

Review Activity 2

Directions: Fill in the chart using **X** for yes and **▬** for no as you solve the puzzle.

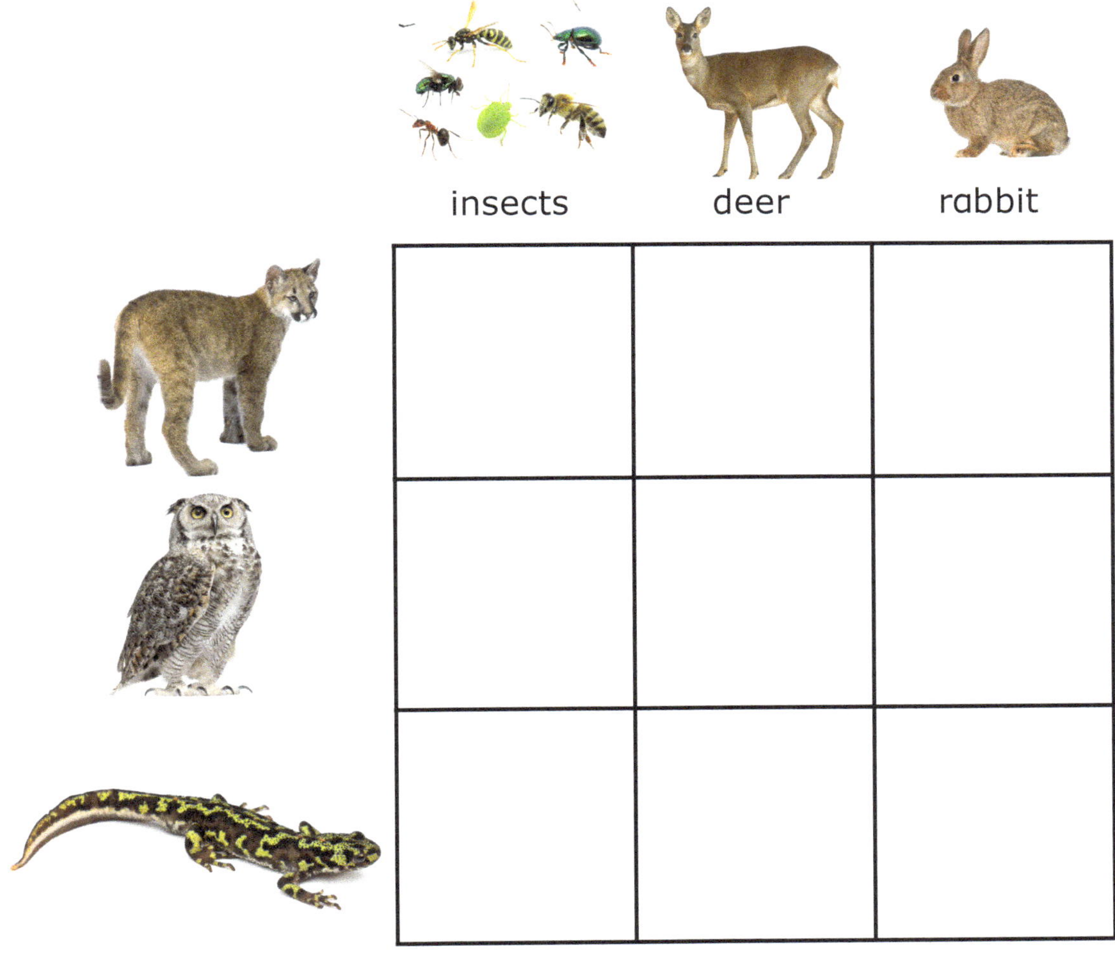

A cougar, a great horned owl, and a newt are carnivores. Find each animal's favorite prey.

1. The amphibian hunts winged prey, but the winged vertebrate favors small mammals with 4 legs.

2. The mammal that preys on the larger mammal uses its long tail for balance as it runs.

Review Activity 3

Directions: Fill in the chart using **X** for yes and **–** for no as you solve the puzzle.

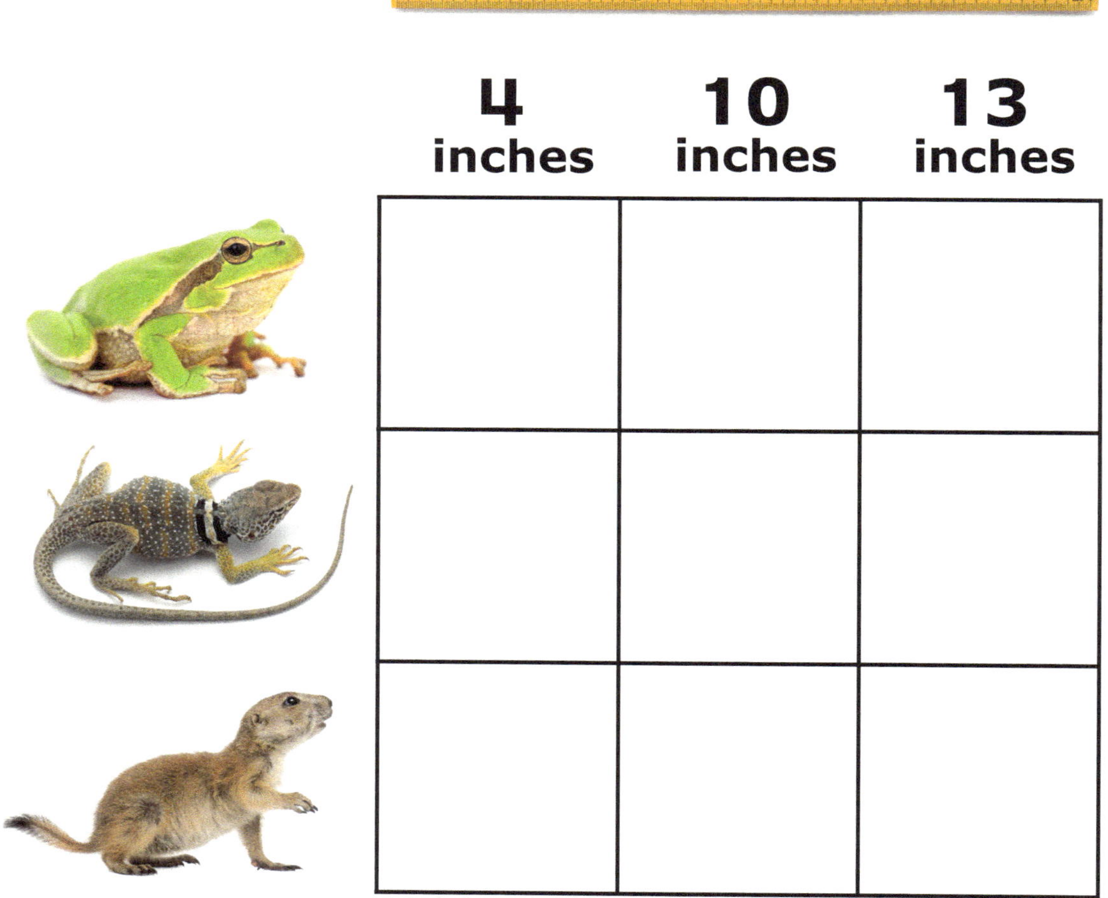

A tree frog, a collared lizard, and a prairie dog grow to be different sizes. Find the length of each animal.

1. The warm blooded vertebrate is larger than the scaly reptile.

2. The amphibian is the smallest.

Review Activity 4

Directions: Fill in the chart using **X** for yes and **–** for no as you solve the puzzle.

A turtle, a flying squirrel, and a roadrunner live in different habitats. Find where each animal lives.

1. The cold blooded animal lives where it can cool off swimming in the water or warm up in the sun.

2. The mammal likes trees more than the bird who runs faster than it flies.

Review Activity 5

Directions: Fill in the chart using **X** for yes and **–** for no as you solve the puzzle.

A polar bear, ostrich, and gorilla all grow to different heights*. Find each animal's height.

1. The mammal that is a carnivore is taller than both herbivores.

2. The vertebrate without hair is taller than one of the mammals.

*For the polar bear and gorilla, this is the height of the animal standing on its hind legs.

Review Activity 6

Directions: Fill in the chart using **X** for yes and **–** for no as you solve the puzzle.

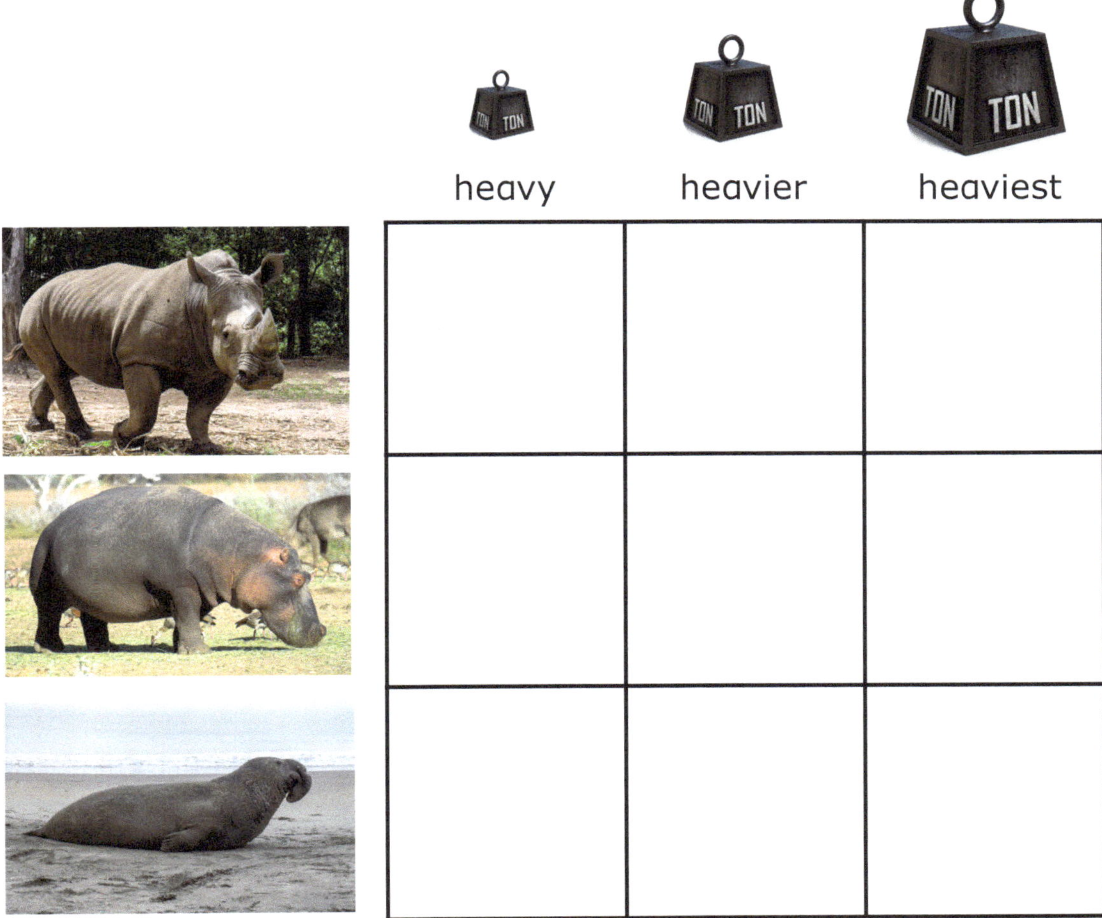

A rhinoceros, hippopotamus, and elephant seal all grow to different weights. Find each animal's weight.

1. The warm blooded vertebrate that is a carnivore is heavier than the two herbivores.

2. The vertebrate with tusks is heavier than the other herbivore.

Glossary

amphibian - cold blooded vertebrates that don't have scales; they live part of their lives in water and part on land

camouflage - hiding or disguising so that an animal's appearance blends in with its surroundings

carnivore - an animal that eats other animals (meat)

clutch - group of eggs delivered at one time

cold blooded - having a body temperature that varies is dependent on the surrounding air or water temperature

environment - The type of area and conditions an animals lives in

exoskeleton - external support or covering for animals without internal bones

fish - cold blooded vertebrate with gills that lays eggs and lives in water; most have scales and fins

gills - the organ animals use to help them breath oxygen underwater

habitat - the type of area and conditions an animal makes its home

hair - helps mammals to maintain body temperature, hide in their environment, and defend themselves; different types include fur, whiskers, wool, fleece, quills, bristles, and guard hairs (such as a mane)

herbivore - an animal that eats plants

insect - an invertebrate with 3 body segments, 6 legs, and 2 antenna, which lays eggs and goes through 4 life stages

invertebrate - an animal that does not have bones or a spine inside its body

mammal - a warm blooded vertebrate that typically has hair, produces milk, and gives birth to live young

omnivore - an animal that eats plants and other animals

poisonous - something that can cause illness or death to a living thing

predator - an animal which hunts another animal to kill or eat

prey - animals that are hunted

reptile - a cold blooded vertebrate that has scales and lays eggs

scale - hard plates which form a protective outer covering for fish and reptiles

venomous - a poison that some animals use to help them catch prey or defend themselves with. Venom is usually passed to the other animal through a bite or sting

vertebrate - an animal that does have bones or a spine inside its body

vocalization - a sound produced by animals to communicate

warm blooded - able to keep up a relatively high constant body temperature that is independent of the surroundings

Answers

Vertebrates and Invertebrates

Activity 1 (p. 3)
1. a vertebrate
2. cats, birds, lizards, fish
3. an invertebrate
4. insects, crabs, snails, spiders, shellfish
5. octopus, jellyfish, worms, slugs

Activity 2 (p. 4)

Activity 3 (p. 5)
1. snail
2. centipede
3. elephant

Activity 4 (p. 6)
1. beetle
2. newt
3. peacock
4. crab

Activity 5 (p. 7)

Activity 6 (p. 8)
1. sea star
2. butterfly
3. squirrel

Activity 7 (p. 9)
1. octopus
2. agama
3. anemone
4. parrot

Review (p. 11)
1. animals
2. vertebrates
3. invertebrates
4. exoskeleton
5. no exoskeleton

Research Question: giant squid

Cold Blooded and Warm Blooded Animals

Activity 1 (p. 13)
1. cold blooded
2. invertebrates
3. spider, shellfish, fish, lizard, shark
4. warm blooded
5. lion, bird, seal

Activity 2 (p. 14)

	savanna	desert	forest
	X 2	— 2	— 1
	— 2	— 2	X 2
	— 2	X 2	— 2

Activity 3 (p. 15)
1. stingray
2. tortoise
3. lemur

Activity 4 (p. 16)
1. penguin
2. tarantula
3. weasel
4. toad

Activity 5 (p. 17)

	2	4	5
	— 2	— 2	X 2
	— 1	X 2	— 2
	X 2	— 2	— 1

Activity 6 (p. 18)
1. sea slug
2. viper
3. butterfly

Activity 7 (p. 19)
1. mouse
2. toad
3. scorpion
4. whale

Review (p. 21)
1. cold blooded
2. warm blooded
3. invertebrates
4. vertebrates

Research Question: The whale shark, which is actually a fish and not a whale.

Mammals and Reptiles

Activity 1 (p. 23)

1st row: reptile, cold blooded, scales; mammal, warm blooded, hair; mammal, warm blooded, hair

2nd row: mammal, warm blooded, hair; mammal, warm blooded, hair; mammal, warm blooded, hair

3rd row: reptile, cold blooded, scales; mammal, warm blooded, hair; reptile, cold blooded, scales

4th row: mammal, warm blooded, hair; reptile, cold blooded, scales; mammal, warm blooded, hair

Activity 2 (p. 24)

	savanna	forest	wetland
	— 1	X 2	— 2
	— 1	— 2	X 2
	X 1	— 1	— 1

Activity 3 (p. 25)
1. snake
2. river otter
3. hedgehog

Activity 4 (p. 26)
1. green anole
2. green tree python
3. narwhal
4. moose

Activity 5 (p. 27)

	tropical jungle	savanna	tundra
	— 1	— 2	X 2
	X 1	— 1	— 1
	— 1	X 2	— 2

Activity 6 (p. 28)
1. fox bat
2. bearded dragon
3. red fox

Activity 7 (p. 29)
1. viper
2. echidna
3. sea turtle
4. humpback whale

Review (p. 31)
1. Warm blooded with hair and four limbs.
2. Cold blooded with bodies covered in scales.

Research Question: Yes, whales do have hair. There are over 80 species of whales, and hair is only visible in some of these species. Hair can be seen on some whales along the jawline on the upper and lower jaw and on top of the head, and around the blowhole. In some adult whales, you can't see hair at all, as some species only have hair when they are in the womb before being born.

Fish and Amphibians

Activity 1 (p. 33)
1. born and live in water; vertebrate
2. born in water, but live on land; vertebrate
3.
4.

Activity 2 (p. 34)

	ocean	tropical jungle	wetland
	— 2	X 2	— 1
	— 1	— 1	X 1
	X 2	— 2	— 1

Activity 3 (p. 35)
1. toad
2. eel
3. salamander

Activity 4 (p. 36)

1. stingray
2. tomato frog
3. fire salamander
4. hammerhead shark

Activity 5 (p. 37)

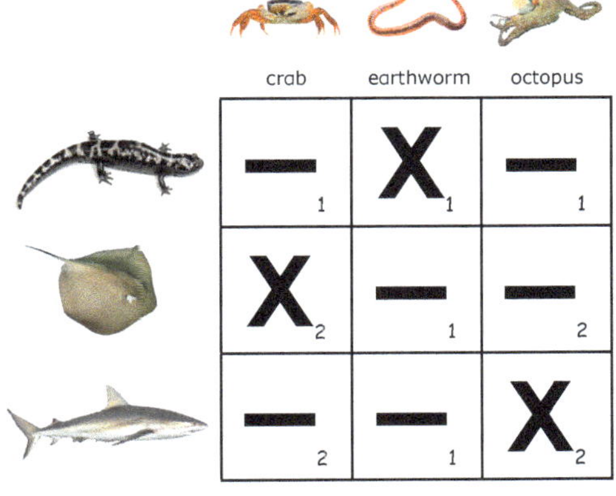

Activity 6 (p. 38)

1. seahorse
2. tadpole
3. arowana

Activity 7 (p. 39)

1. newt larva
2. salamander
3. sturgeon
4. sturgeon fry

Review (p. 41)

1. Fish are cold blooded vertebrates that spend their entire life in water.
2. Amphibians are cold blooded vertebrates that begin life in water but live on land as adults.

Thinker Question: The animal has a pair of legs, so it is not a fish. Fish spend their entire life in water, but amphibians begin life in water, but spend much of their adult life on land.

Research Question: Fish and amphibians lay hundreds or thousands of eggs because 1) the number of eggs and developing young that are eaten by predators and 2) the eggs are fertilized externally so not all eggs are fertilized.

Carnivores, Herbivores, and Omnivores

Activity 1 (p. 43)

1. carnivore, herbivore, omnivore
2. herbivore, omnivore, carnivore
3. omnivore, herbivore, carnivore
4. herbivore, carnivore, omnivore

Activity 2 (p. 44)

Activity 3 (p. 45)

1. millipede
2. Komodo dragon
3. pipefish

Activity 4 (p. 46)

1. tarantula
2. pit viper
3. sea star
4. three-toed sloth

Activity 5 (p. 47)

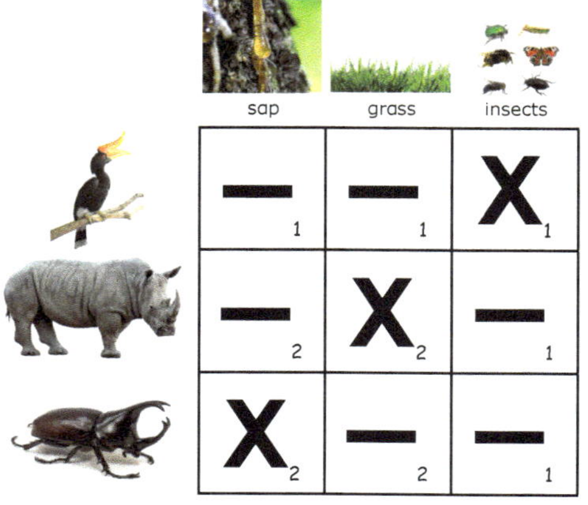

Activity 6 (p. 48)

1. sea urchin
2. hummingbird
3. toad

Activity 7 (p. 49)

1. ring-tailed lemur
2. lion
3. ostrich
4. poison dart frog

Review (p. 51)

Thinker Question: Yes, for example, a raccoon is an omnivore and a bullfrog is a carnivore, but a raccoon will eat a bullfrog.

Research Question: kodiak (brown) bear

Types of Birds

Activity 1 (p. 53)

1. 1st row: water bird, water bird, song bird
   2nd row: bird of prey, song bird, bird of prey
2. 1st row: song bird, water bird, water bird, bird of prey
   2nd row: water bird, bird of prey, bird of prey, song bird

Research Question: The largest bird in the world is the ostrich. The birds that cannot fly include ostrich, emu, rhea, kiwi, cassowary, and penguins.

Activity 2 (p. 54)

Activity 3 (p. 55)

1. robin
2. mallard duck
3. buzzard

Activity 4 (p. 56)

1. thrush
2. great horned owl
3. goose
4. stork

Activity 5 (p. 57)

	4 years	15 years	20 years
	— 1	— 2	X 2
	X 1	— 1	— 1
	— 1	X 2	— 2

Activity 6 (p. 58)

1. turkey vulture
2. phoebe
3. goose

Activity 7 (p. 59)

1. finch
2. kestrel
3. seagull
4. pelican

Review (p. 61)

1. song bird, vertebrate, warm blooded, small, no webbed feet, no talons, omnivore
2. water bird, vertebrate, warm blooded, small and large, webbed feet, no talons
3. bird of prey, vertebrate, warm blooded, small and large, no webbed feet, talons, carnivore

Research Question: No, some water birds are omnivores. For example, seagulls, ducks, swans, and cranes are all omnivores. Examples of carnivorous water birds include herons, kingfishers, and egrets.

Camouflage

Activity 1 (p. 63)

polar bears eat seals, praying mantis eat caterpillars and grass hoppers, gopher snakes eat chipmunks and gophers, leopards eat warthogs and hare, wolf spiders eat beetles and caterpillar.

Activity 2 (p. 64)

1. jaguar
2. lizard
3. moth

Activity 3 (p. 65)

1. silky shark
2. rabbit
3. sea turtle
4. owl

Activity 4 (p. 66)

1. spider
2. katydid leafbug
3. sole

Activity 5 (p. 67)

1. reef octopus
2. chipmunk
3. spider
4. woodcock

Review (p. 69)

Review

Activity 1 (p. 70)

Activity 2 (p. 71)

Activity 3 (p. 72)

Activity 4 (p. 73)

Activity 5 (p. 74)

Activity 6 (p. 75)